ems should be returned on or before the last date
own below. Items not already requested by other
orrowers may be renewed in person, in writing or by
lephone. To renew, please quote the number on the
rcode label. To renew online a PIN is required.
his can be requested at your local library.
enew online @ **www.dublincitypubliclibraries.ie**
nes charged for overdue items will include postage
curred in recovery. Damage to or loss of items will
e charged to the borrower.

Leabharlanna Poiblí Chathair Bhaile Átha Cliath
Dublin City Public Libraries

Dublin City
Baile Átha Cliath

Drumcondra Branch Tel. 8377206

Nelson Mandela

...and his struggle for freedom

Sarah Ridley

W

FRANKLIN WATTS

LONDON • SYDNEY

First published in 2009 by
Franklin Watts
338 Euston Road
London NW1 3BH

Franklin Watts Australia
Hachette Children's Books
Level 17/207 Kent Street
Sydney NSW 2000

Copyright © Franklin Watts 2009

ISBN 978 0 7496 8711 3
Dewey classification: 968.06'5'092

Series Editor: Jeremy Smith
Art Director: Jonathan Hair
Design: Simon Morse
Cover Design: Jonathan Hair
Picture Research: Sarah Ridley

Picture credits: African Pictures/AKG
Images: front cover, 1, 2, 10, 13, 14,15, 20.
Walter Dhladhla/AFP/Getty Images: 22.
Denis Farrell/AP/PA/Photos: 8. Fox
Photos/Hulton Archive/Getty Images: 6.
Themba Hadebe/AFP/Getty Images: 23.
Roger de Harpe/Gallo/Corbis: 7, 17. Hulton
Archive/Getty Images: 5. Peter
Johnson/Corbis: 4. Keystone/Getty Images:
16. Gideon Mendel/AFP/Getty Images: 19.
Per Anders Pettersson/Liaison/Getty
Images: 21. Hart Preston/Time Life/Getty
Images: 11. Three Lions/Hulton
Archive/Getty Images: 12.
Ullstein/Topfoto: 18. Margaret Bourke-
White/Time Life/Getty Images: 9.

Every attempt has been made to clear
copyright. Should there be any
inadvertent omission please apply to the
publisher for rectification.

A CIP catalogue record for this book is
available from the British Library

Franklin Watts is a division of Hachette
Children's Books, an Hachette UK company.
www.hachette.co.uk

Printed in China

Contents

Early life

Nelson Mandela was born on 18 July 1918, in South Africa. He was named Rolihlahla by his parents. His father was an African chief.

▲ Nelson lived in a hut similar to this one.

1902 ▶

Britain wins the Second Boer War in South Africa.

1910 ▶

Britain allows white South Africans to rule themselves.

▲ Workers at a South African mine. White South Africans became rich from the hard work of black African workers.

For several hundred years, white people had taken over land in South Africa that had once belonged to black Africans. By 1910, white South Africans held all the power.

1914-1918 ▶	18 July 1918
The First World War.	Rolihlahla (later Nelson) Mandela is born.

Growing up

At the age of seven, Rolihlahla started school. The teacher gave all her new pupils an English name. This is how Rolihlahla gained the name 'Nelson'.

◄ The school was run by the Church, as here.

1923 ▶

The Native National Congress (formed in 1912) changes its name to African National Congress.

1925 ▶

Nelson Mandela starts school.

Like many boys from the rural district of Thembuland, Nelson loved to stick fight, just like these South Africans are doing here.

Two years later, Nelson's father died and he went to live with Chief Jongintaba Dalindyebo. The Chief treated Nelson the same as his own son, Justice. Nelson went to school and then on to university.

1927 ▶

Nelson's father dies. Nelson goes to live with Chief Jongintaba.

1939 ▶

Nelson goes to Fort Hare University.

To Johannesburg

After a disagreement at university, Nelson had to leave without finishing his studies. The Chief was not pleased. He tried to arrange marriages for Nelson and Justice, but they ran away to Johannesburg.

This photo shows Nelson (centre back) at about the age of 19.

1939 ▶

The Second World War starts.

February
1940 ▶

Nelson moves to the city of Johannesburg.

Nelson and Justice found jobs working for a gold mine where Nelson was a security guard. After a few months he found a new job in a law office.

Black African gold miners worked long hours in terrible heat, for small wages.

1941

Nelson starts work in a law office.

Work

During the day, Nelson worked in the law office. He was one of only two black people in the office. At night he studied for a law degree.

▶ Nelson met Walter Sisulu in 1941 while working in Sisulu's law office. They were to become friends for life.

1942 ▶

Nelson finishes his university degree by post and begins a law degree.

Many black South Africans lived in extremely poor conditions.

Nelson could see how unfair life was for many black South Africans. Even though there were millions of blacks, the white people had most of the important jobs, good houses, schools and healthcare.

1942

Nelson joins the African National Congress (ANC).

1944

Nelson marries Evelyn Mase.

The ANC

Nelson now belonged to an organisation called the African National Congress (ANC). The ANC wanted black and white South Africans to be treated the same.

Only white children were allowed to play in this pond.

1945 ▶

The Second World War ends.

1948 ▶

The Afrikaner National Party takes power in South Africa.

12

But in 1948, new laws made life even more difficult for black people. Blacks and whites had to live in different areas of towns or cities, and live separate lives. Black South Africans were not allowed to vote.

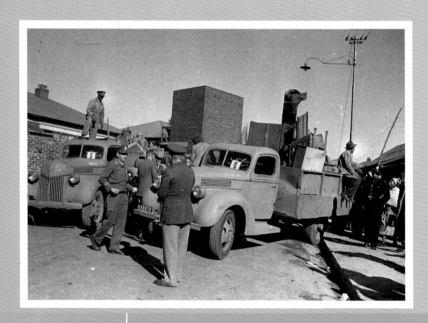

Black families leave Sophiatown in 1955. They had to move to a 'blacks only' area.

1948 onwards

New laws separate black and white South Africans in all areas of life. This is called apartheid, which means 'apartness'.

13

Meetings and marches

Nelson and his friends decided to protest against these new laws and to force the government to give equal rights to all South Africans.

◀ Nelson and the ANC organised protests against the new apartheid laws.

1950 ▶

Nelson becomes an ANC leader.

June
1952 ▶

The ANC starts its Defiance Campaign, joining forces with other non-white South Africans to fight for change.

The government could see that the ANC had a lot of support. They reacted by making life even worse for black South Africans. They banned Nelson from going to meetings.

Nelson in his law office. Nelson worked so hard that his family hardly saw him.

July
1952

Nelson is banned from meetings and is not allowed to leave Johannesburg.

August
1952

Nelson opens his own law office.

15

Violent struggle

The government often used force against the ANC. Nelson decided it was time to set up another group that would use bomb attacks on important buildings to get change.

At this time, Nelson married Winnie Madikizela.

1956	1957	1958	March 1960
Nelson is arrested but walks free.	Nelson and Evelyn are divorced.	Nelson marries Winnie Madikizela.	Sharpeville massacre. Police kill 69 people.

Now the government was searching for Nelson. Eventually, in 1962, the government tracked him down, arrested him, took him to court and sent him to prison.

Robben Island, where Nelson was sent to prison.

April
1960

The ANC is outlawed.

1963-1964

Nelson and others are found guilty of organising bomb attacks between 1961-1962.

Prison life

Prison life was hard. Nelson led protests for better food and treatment for the prisoners. Over the next 27 years, he hardly saw his wife or any of his children.

Nelson and other prisoners had to break stones for hours.

1964 ▶

Nelson enters Robben Island Prison.

18

1968 ▶

Nelson cannot attend his mother's funeral.

More and more people around the world began to fight for Nelson's release. As a result, prison staff took better care of him. After 18 years he moved to Pollsmoor Prison where conditions were better.

Many people protested about Nelson's imprisonment.

1969

Nelson's eldest son dies in a car accident.

1976

Black children are killed in a protest at Soweto.

1980

Oliver Tambo starts a campaign to free Nelson.

19

Freedom

After 27 years in prison, Nelson walked free on 11 February 1990. Almost immediately he began to lead the ANC again and work for equal rights for all South Africans.

Nelson and his wife, Winnie, gave the ANC salute as he walked free.

February
1990
President FW de Klerk lifts the ban on the ANC.

February
1990
Nelson is released from prison.

1992
Nelson divorces Winnie Mandela.

Nelson votes in the first free election in South Africa. At last, every adult could vote, whatever the colour of their skin.

It was a struggle to get all the African people to work together and to persuade the white government that it was time for change. But, in 1994, Nelson became President of South Africa.

1993

Nelson and FW de Klerk win the Nobel Peace Prize.

1994

Nelson becomes President of South Africa, aged 75.

1998

Nelson marries Graca Machel.

Retirement

During his five years as president, Nelson helped lead South Africa through some difficult times. He settled arguments between many groups of people in the country.

Archbishop Desmond Tutu and Nelson Mandela helped people recover from some of the terrible events in South Africa.

1998

Truth and Reconciliation Commission ends.

1999

Nelson steps down as president.

2000

Nelson begins to raise awareness of AIDS.

In 1999, Nelson retired. He went to live in the village where he grew up, with his third wife Graca. He continues to help others but lives a quieter life.

Nelson celebrated his 90th birthday with Graca and his family.

2004

Nelson retires from public life.

2008

Nelson's 90th birthday.

23

Glossary

AIDS A serious disease that attacks the body's defences.

Afrikaner National Party Political party in South Africa that supported apartheid (see below).

Apartheid The laws that existed in South Africa between 1948 and 1990 to keep whites and blacks apart.

Ban Forbid someone from doing something.

Chief An important person in an African community.

Equal rights Where everyone is treated the same and has the same chances in life.

Laws Rules made by a government. Lawyers help people understand and live within the law.

President The political leader of a country.

Truth and Reconciliation Council The Truth and Reconciliation Commission investigated crimes committed in South Africa during the apartheid era.

Index